THE JASON DONOVAN FILE

Also by Neil Wallis and Dave Hogan
The Neighbours Factfile

THE JASON DONOVAN FILE

*Everything you always wanted
to know about the
actor, singer and superstar*

NEIL WALLIS
AND
DAVE HOGAN

ANGUS & ROBERTSON PUBLISHERS

16 Golden Square, London W1R 4BN,
United Kingdom and
Unit 4, Eden Park, 31 Waterloo Road,
North Ryde, NSW, Australia 2113.

First published in the United Kingdom by
Angus & Robertson (UK) in 1989
First published in Australia by
Angus & Robertson Publishers in 1990

Reprinted 1989

British Library Cataloguing in Publication Data

Wallis, Neil
    The Jason Donovan file : everything you always wanted
    to know about the actor, singer and superstar!
    1. Television drama. Acting. Donovan, Jason
    I. Title   II. Hogan, Dave
    791.45'028'0924

ISBN 0 207 16575 0

Typeset in Great Britain by
AKM Associates (UK) Ltd, Southall, London
Printed in Great Britain by
Scotprint Ltd, Musselburgh, Scotland

CONTENTS

1
FROM SMALL
BEGINNINGS . . .

Jason Donovan was born on 1 June 1968 at the Francis
Xavier Cabrini Hospital in Malvern, Melbourne, Australia,
and came into the world screaming his head off and
weighing 8lbs 4ozs. He looked, says his dad Terence
Donovan, 'like a miniature version of a fat Japanese
Sumo wrestler'.

He was christened Jason after the hero of the
Greek legends 'Jason and the Argonauts' because his
mother Sue had been reading a play about the ancient
hero and fallen in love with the name. And just as he was
named after a hero, that ordinary little baby went on to
become a hero to millions of youngsters worldwide, first
as happy-go-lucky Scott in the world-beating TV soap
opera 'Neighbours', and then later in his own right as a
smash-hit popsinger.

But there was very little in his early life to indicate

the glorious future that he had ahead of him. If anything, he was most noticeable during his school years for *not* being remarkable. And he certainly wasn't the sort of rascal that most of his classmates became. As he was later to recall: 'I never particularly liked school but I thought that if you had to be there then you might as well make the best of it. And to me that meant working hard when required and doing all that was necessary with the minimum of fuss. I really objected when the other kids disrupted lessons because it was so unfair to those who did want to work. If they hated it so much why didn't they simply play truant – just like I did on the odd occasion when a particular lesson got too much for me.'

Because his parents split up when he was very young, Jason went to school earlier than most children – but not without a fight! He only lasted one day at kindergarten because he cried and screamed so much that he was sick, and he never relented all day until the moment his father appeared. He never went back. Even at infants school he regularly had tantrums so he could be sent home, but his father would have none of it and forced him to stay at school.

From primary school Jason went to the local Spring Road School in Malvern, then when he was fifteen he sat the entrance exam for De La Salle College, the local Catholic high school. Despite his Irish background he isn't in fact Catholic, but De La Salle was simply the best local school and his father was always determined that Jason should get the best start in life possible. On the first try Jason failed to get in and has never forgotten his sense of failure, humiliation and shame at letting his

Crest of De La Salle College, where Jason did his
Higher School Certificate, the Australian equivalent
of Britain's 'A' levels

father down, so he worked hard and passed the second
time around.

A classmate from those days at De La Salle, now
working as a bellboy at a Melbourne hotel, remembers
the young Jason: 'He was pretty much of a nonentity at

school, he didn't really seem to have any close pals or be in any of the gangs. But when I look back it wasn't that no one liked him, more that Jason couldn't be bothered with most lads of his own age because he found us all a bit juvenile then. Not that he was a wimp, he had quite a few fights with other lads just like everyone else, but he used to prefer to tag around with older blokes. Even then he was a knockout with the girls. I remember we were all very amazed and envious when we discovered he'd been going out with an *older* girl from Killdara Catholic Girls' School just over the road from our school. We were all very jealous.'

The schoolfriend went on: 'He only really had one mate in our year, James Maguire, who lived quite near Jason. But even then Jason kept him at arm's length and for some reason wouldn't allow him to call for him or go round to his place. But funnily enough, it was after James ignored all that and went round anyway that they became really close. They became inseparable, used to cycle to school together, started missing lessons to go into Melbourne to mess around. I think they even both made themselves ill together when they tried smoking cigarettes for the first time behind the bike sheds. They still are close, all these years later.'

It was at this time that, like many Australian kids, Jason became hooked on surfing. On many an occasion he would sneak out of his dad's house before dawn, pick up his trusty Malibu surfboard, meet up with James or other pals, and head off to one of Melbourne's many superb surfing beaches. 'The best waves are at dawn in the morning', explained Jason, 'and that's when the beaches are most deserted. It is a fabulous experience. Even now it's the sport I like most – at one stage I got good enough to enter championships, though I never won anything. And one of my best pals to this day is one of Australia's top surfers.'

The bad news about those early morning surfing trips was that if the water was good then they would very often last all day. He'd forget about school altogether until it was too late to go, or turn up so late for class that he'd get sent home in disgrace or have to stay behind. And that led to more trouble with his father.

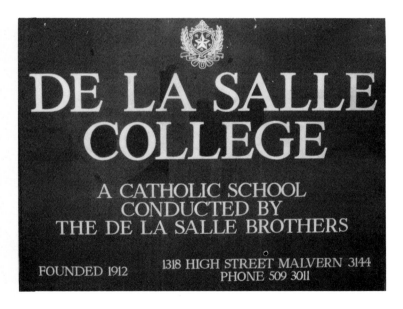

DE LA SALLE COLLEGE

A CATHOLIC SCHOOL CONDUCTED BY THE DE LA SALLE BROTHERS

FOUNDED 1912

1318 HIGH STREET MALVERN 3144
PHONE 509 3011

His interest in music – which has propelled him to pop stardom – began in those early schooldays. His father Terence Donovan said, 'I once actually released a pop ballad which did well in Australia. Music has always run in my family and Jason was no exception. In fact I always thought it could well become a career for him. When he was nine I enrolled him in the Melbourne Conservatory of Music. He also joined the Australian Boys' Choir for about five years. At the same time I had him having piano lessons. Music turned out to be one of his best subjects at school.

'We often used to play the piano together. He also taught himself to play guitar, and as a teenager he became very into heavy metal and punk music. Not so long ago he admitted to me that he used to sneak out into Melbourne to go to rock clubs. He wanted me to buy him a set of drums at one stage so he could become a rock drummer. Thankfully, I talked him out of that one!'

Jason's school, De La Salle College

A picture from Jason's school magazine. He is
second from left, front row

But despite all the distractions of these outside
interests – plus another one called acting, about which
more later – his teachers remember him as a bright kid.
He made an effort to get all his projects done on time and
was a fanatic about neatness. The problem was, recall
teachers at De La Salle, that he did exactly what was
required, no more and no less. With the result that as his
final school exams loomed (the Higher School Certificate, Australia's version of A Levels) he was warned that
he would probably fail.

So, typically singlemindedly, he moved out of his
father's house to avoid distractions, like his record player
and friends calling by, and in with his grandmother.
There he spent eighteen hours a day for two weeks going
through the whole two year curriculum and revising for

the exams. No one thought he could do it. Jason knew that he could.

When the results came out Jason was the only one not to be surprised that he had passed every subject – English, Economics, Politics, Art and Accounting. He had amassed 285 out of a possible 410 points. Last year he said in an interview: 'I knew that if I didn't pass first time then my dad would insist that I stay on and resit. I also knew that I would probably agree, purely because I hate to let *anything* beat me if I can possibly avoid it. And I knew I was capable of passing anyway. I also knew that I was ready to leave school. The wide world was beckoning.'

He had no idea exactly what was in store, though. Jason, who once had thoughts of becoming a plumber, then thought his career probably lay in the direction of Art. An excellent painter and draughtsman, he thought he would make a living in the advertising world. But then one day he came home to find a message asking him to telephone Australia's Grundy Television. They wanted to talk to him about auditioning for a part in a soap opera called 'Neighbours'. . . .

2

FAMILY AT WAR

The most significant single event of Jason Donovan's life happened when he was just five years old. That was when his beautiful young mother Sue decided to walk out on him and his father Terence and run off with another man.

It was an agonising time for the bewildered and frightened child, and led to much heartache and anguish in the years that followed. But, in the long run, there were plus sides too. For Jason's single-parent father Terry was an actor who had no option but to take Jason along with him whenever and wherever he worked. His son grew up at ease in the showbusiness world, not over-awed by it, and despite his rocket-like elevation to being a worldwide superstar he has managed to keep both feet very firmly on the ground and not get swept away by the gloss and glitter that has time and again been the

Terence Donovan and first wife Sue soon after their wedding

downfall of much older and less successful performers.

All those years of living alone together and having to rely on each other also formed an unshakeable rock-like bond between father and son, which has also given Jason a sense of security and strength that most youngsters would envy.

Terry Donovan was born in Middlesex, England, and still has three brothers in Britain. He emigrated to Australia when he was a young man and soon established himself as a talented actor. So much so that he decided to return to Britain to try to achieve stardom there. He had recently started going out with an actress girlfriend called Sue McIntosh. When he decided to go to Britain he asked her to marry him and come with him. On impulse, and swept off her feet by her handsome lover, she agreed.

It was a decision that was to lead to much heartbreak and distress in the years that followed. In Britain both achieved reasonable success, and in fact Sue was for a while one of Benny Hill's 'Angels' on TV. But neither achieved real stardom and they decided to return to Australia. There Sue soon found work as an actress in comic star Paul Hogan's TV shows and as a presenter and newsreader. Terry also found much stage and television work. Then only child Jason was born – but the marriage was already in trouble. After struggling to work things out, Sue finally fell for a handsome young TV producer called John McIntosh and walked out on both Terry and Jason. It was a tough decision – but what hurt Jason most in the years to come was that even though she set up home just a couple of miles away she virtually cut off all contact with her son.

Terry never forgave her – and neither, for many years, did Jason. Terry spoke last year of the heartbreak – but also the happiness – of having to rear his son alone, of having to give him love and security to make up for losing his mother, while keeping an acting career going to ensure they had a roof over their heads.

'It was tough', Terry recalls, 'we had to survive as best we could, but it was difficult in almost every way you can imagine. Financially, there were times when we struggled. I remember having to go home to tell him one day that a TV series I was appearing in had ended and there was no work on the horizon. That can be frightening for a lad. I spent a lot of time out of work and on the dole, but I was determined he would suffer as little as possible. It wouldn't have been so bad if I'd had a partner, family, to look after Jason so I could take acting jobs away, but I didn't. I had to fit my work in around his schooling, or take him with me.'

But then Terry's mother flew out from England to move in with them and make life easier. As Terry said, 'She became a second mother to Jason, he worshipped her. It made his life fuller, he needed a woman's influence as well as mine and they became very close. But then she went into hospital for a fairly routine operation and the day before we were due to pick her up to bring her home, we got a call to say she'd had a heart attack and died. Jason was devastated. She was eighty-one, so it wasn't such a shock to me, but when you are ten you don't expect death and can't be philosophical about it.

Jason aged two with young mum Sue McIntosh
and much-loved rocking horse. Just months later,
Sue walked out on Jason and his father

'Despite his distress, he never saw more of his mother. Occasional birthdays and Christmases apart, he saw virtually nothing of her. She chose to cut her son right off. I wanted her to have access to him, but she didn't seem to want it. I did my best, but it is not easy being deserted by your mum as a nipper and having only a dad for eight years.'

Terry put all his non-working time into bringing up Jason: 'I was very wary about dominating Jason. I wanted him to develop his own interests and hobbies rather than simply have mine dinned into his head. I wanted him to be himself, not a clone of me. So to start him off swimming or playing tennis I didn't order him to give them a go, I told him I was going to give those sports a bash and did he fancy joining in? Sometimes, he said no, usually he said yes – and I am proud that to this day he is very keen on sport and keeping fit.'

Those times left Jason with a very sensible attitude towards money. 'We had a lot of financial insecurity in those days, but we coped. I remember being out of work and having to scrimp and save like mad to buy him a bike for Christmas because every other kid on the block had one. I wasn't having my Jason left out.

'We could never afford holidays, except for the time a film project came good. I had to go to Hollywood on business and got together enough cash to take Jason with me. Then through the studio I got us free tickets to Disneyland – he had a ball, it was wonderful for us.'

During this time Sue married John McIntosh. Jason didn't attend the wedding. As years went by he

Jason's father Terence Donovan is one of
Australia's best-known and most respected actors.
As Jason himself says, 'If I've got good looks, you
can see where they come from'

learnt almost by chance that he had gained three half-
sisters from his mother's second marriage. Though he
virtually never heard from his mother, he had to suffer
the distress of turning on the TV and seeing her reading
the news or presenting a show.

Then Jason suffered yet more disruption to his home life: he nearly broke his heart when his father at last fell in love again and decided to remarry. Jason's stepmother is a beautiful redheaded model called Marlene Saunders, but it took Jason quite a while to come to terms with having a new 'mum' and having to share his father's affections and attentions.

As Terry said, 'Suddenly there was this other person taking up some of my time and he couldn't help but be jealous at first. He was twelve, which is anyway a difficult age. Marlene warned me it would be tough, but I naïvely didn't believe her. And it could have gone very sour indeed. Since he was a toddler he had had to learn to wash his own clothes, prepare his own breakfast, do things around the house in his own way. Suddenly there was this woman wanting to do it for him and with her own ways of doing things. That was tough, but eventually we all became very close – and then his little brother Paul came along and he was delighted.'

Jason was in fact best man at his own father's wedding. 'I knew it was vital he didn't feel left out at the wedding, and anyway he genuinely *was* my best friend. And at least I knew he wouldn't roll up drunk! I felt so proud of him, in a smart new suit, that I quite forgot my own nerves. Then came the moment in the service when he was supposed to give me the ring – and couldn't find it! He was mortified, the poor little devil, and began frantically rummaging through his pockets in panic. Everyone except him was falling about laughing, even me and Marlene. Eventually we found it in a tiny corner of an inside pocket where he had put it for safekeeping.

He was really red-faced, but whenever we think of the wedding we remember that bit of it and have a good laugh together.'

Ever since, Jason has been very close to his second mother. Even though he has bought his own house, he still regards Terry and Marlene's place in Melbourne's Armadale suburb as home. And Terry stresses that however rich and famous his son becomes, it will always remain that way.

'This is his sanctuary,' says Terry proudly. 'Whenever he needs a break from the pressure or a good plain homecooked meal – though he can cook a mean omelette himself – he comes running. He plays with his little brother, takes him to school and collects him, and just enjoys being part of an ordinary family. It's something he was robbed of as a child. I am just so glad I can give it to him now.'

3
THE BIG BREAK

Jason Donovan was *not* supposed to become a star. Or even enter showbiz, for that matter. The role of Scott Robinson in 'Neighbours' that was to rocket him to international fame was originally created specifically for another much more experienced actor called Darius Perkins. And Jason himself had already turned down another part in the show. Not only that, but 'Neighbours' was then axed as a failure! But fate had decided that Jason Donovan was going to be a star whether he liked it or not. First 'Neighbours' was unprecedentedly brought back to life by another TV channel, then Perkins was fired from the part of Scott, and finally the show's bosses persuaded Jason to take on the role. And just as importantly, they persuaded Terry that Jason should take on the role. For a close look at Jason's career proves that what happened over 'Neighbours' was typical of the way

The new Scott soon became a great favourite with
the ever-increasing band of 'Neighbours' fans

father and son seemed to do almost everything they
could to ensure the youngster ended up in oblivion as a
plumber or electrician rather than one of the world's
biggest young stars!

Terry Donovan admits with a wry laugh, 'I really
didn't want him in the business and did all I could to put
him off the idea. I did a pretty good job, too. Whenever I
took Jason along with me to TV studios or film sets I
would ensure he saw the boring side rather than the
exciting side, and I have no doubt that he was totally
unimpressed by the business. So it wasn't very difficult to
get him to say no when I started getting asked by TV

people if they could "borrow" Jason for this small part or that walk-on role. I always tried to talk him out of it because it was such an insecure business – he knew that anyway from seeing the number of times I was out of work.

'But then when he was eleven he started to badger me with his interest – and I'd been getting a bit bothered that he was becoming shy and not wanting to go to school. It seemed a way to kill two birds with one stone when a TV company I was working for asked me if I had any ideas of who could play the part of a young boy for a children's programme they were making called "Skyways", a sort of soap opera based around an airline. I asked Jason if he was interested, and he hummed and hawed. But when I told him it would get him a few days off school and he'd get paid he went for it.'

A co-star for Jason on the show was a little girl called Kylie Minogue. Recently they sat down together to watch a video of some of the old episodes: 'I was both impressed and horrified,' says Jason now. 'I thought it was quite well done, but I was so tubby! I was like a little fat-faced ball with this dreadful basin-cut hair. Yuk!' But even then Kylie thought he was cute. . . .

From then on Jason never seemed to be out of work as a child actor – though he still wasn't starry-eyed. As Terry says, 'By the time he was thirteen we often went to work together to record whatever series we were in. We would be testing each other's lines, making sure we both had our travelling arrangements and eating times sorted out, checking when we'd finish work. I never encouraged him to see it as a career, far from it, I just insisted that in acting as in everything else that he should do it as well as possible. And he obviously did do well, didn't he?'

'Skyways' led onto another string of children's programmes, but even so Jason decided to drop all acting during his final year before his vital HSC exams. Which was just when Australia's Grundy Television came knocking on his door to offer him his first role in an adult show – it was that new soap opera called 'Neighbours'.

The part was the plum role of Danny Ramsay, son of Madge Mitchell's brother and cousin to Scott, the role earmarked for twenty-year-old established young actor Darius Perkins. Jason, then barely seventeen, admits he was tempted – after all, he was getting to the age when he had to decide on his career, and a job like this could have taken the decision out of his hands. But he knew just how insecure acting is – and, after consulting his dad and his grandmother, decided to turn down the role as Danny and stick at school. Just after he took – and passed – those vital exams the show was axed. When it was revived some months later the phone rang – it was the Grundy casting director who now wanted him to play Scott. They were also offering much more money. This time both Jason and his father knew it was time to grab the opportunity with both hands.

Terry just 'felt that he was fated to join the show. The part was tailor-made for him, and he had seen enough of the acting game not to fall into the same trap as his poor predecessor had.'

Darius Perkins has never hidden the fact that he felt he blew his big chance. He has gone out of his way to talk about it to warn other young actors of the pitfalls and dangers of sudden massive TV exposure. He admits, 'I let all the attention and fame go to my head. I started to believe my own publicity, the hype, and think it was true. I forgot it was simply a soap opera – even though a good one – and began to think I was as wonderful as everyone told me I was. And I began to lose my own sense of identity. People thought I really *was* Scott and treated me and talked to me accordingly. It was as if Darius Perkins didn't exist, only this creature Scott Robinson.'

He started to turn up late for work, began to delay shooting, began to get accused of being uncooperative. So when it was decided to revive the show after its sudden axing, he was dropped as Scott and Jason was given the part. Darius didn't work for another eighteen months, and has never regained the stardom he achieved with 'Neighbours'. 'I am older and wiser now. But I am very impressed with how Jason has handled himself. He has a maturity far beyond his years. It is tough being Scott, but he has done it brilliantly *and* handled the fame and stardom without a problem. I take my hat off to him. He is a star and deserves to be.'

But as Jason himself once said, 'It is such damn hard work that you either love it or it will become a nightmare and drive you mad. Not least because it takes up so much of your time. You are at the set most days from 7am to 7pm, sometimes for just a few minutes dialogue in the episode. The rest of the time you're having to learn tomorrow's lines. Time off doesn't seem to exist. Your private life becomes non-existent.

'You try to become pals with the rest of the cast,

Soon after joining Neighbours as 'Scott', Jason
clowns around on his skateboard still wearing his
old De La Salle College cap

but frankly you are together so much at the studio that you don't want to see the same bunch socially after work as well. And it's hard to keep up your old social life, because your ordinary friends don't understand why you can't just drop everything to run off to a good party or see a hot film. So you can very quickly lose contact with ordinary people. I was lucky because I'd lived around that all my life because of dad, and he made sure I didn't fall into the same trap. I am proud that all my close friends now are the same as the ones I had when I left school and started in "Neighbours".'

Not that it is all hard work. Jason has very fond memories of his time on the set of 'Neighbours'. He formed a particularly close friendship with co-star Peter O'Brien, and they would often fool around arm-wrestling and playing board games together. They were the exception to the rule, and would socialise after work. Jason also became pals with Guy Pearce – they began to bring guitars in and would sit and sing pop songs together. Then Craig McLachlan was the next new signing, and he too was music mad. He was also a practical joker and he and Jason spent months planning and executing elaborate japes against each other – which somehow used to always end up with one or the other being soaked or covered in muck.

Jason also became close to two of the older women in the show. One was Anne Charleston, who plays his screen mother-in-law Madge Mitchell. The other was Myra de Groot, who played Des Clarke's interfering mother Eileen Clarke. He was devastated two years later when she suddenly died of cancer.

However, it was in his first few weeks on 'Neighbours' that he came face to face with a vaguely familiar, small but strikingly pretty bright-eyed blonde girl of about his age. It was as they boarded a minibus to take them from the Nunawading studios of Australia's Channel Ten Network – where 'Neighbours' is filmed – out to the actual street where they do the outside shots. She sat next to him, nudged him in the ribs and said: 'Hi, Jas, remember me?' He confesses that at first his mind was a blank. But then she reminded him that they had been co-stars as children in a programme called 'Skyways'. Then he remembered her name and started chatting. She was Kylie Minogue.

4

THE TRUTH ABOUT JASON AND KYLIE

The Jason Donovan story cannot be told properly without the name Kylie Minogue featuring in it very prominently. She, as everyone in the world must now know, first found fame as an actress playing opposite Jason in 'Neighbours' as his screen girlfriend (later his wife) Charlene. They were a dynamic double-act who are largely credited with giving the smash-hit show its massive appeal among youngsters. Very quickly, rumours began to circulate first in showbiz circles and later in the media that they had begun a real-life romance. And as the careers of each of them blossomed to the point where they both became international acting and singing stars, the romance rumours gathered pace. Rumours which, as most people know, both Jason and Kylie have totally denied. They are simply good friends, they insist. So just what is the truth?

A record company executive explained the situation thus, 'Simply as singing stars, there is endless worldwide speculation that Jason and Kylie are going to make an album together, appear in concert together, go on tour together. We are offered ever-increasing amounts of cash to make that happen. But unless they desperately need the money or sudden massive exposure they won't do it. Why? Because the event would simply be an unrepeatable one-off, and doing it would kill off all those valuable will-they-won't-they stories. The same thing applies to the romance stories. As long as they both deny them, and don't get caught moving in with each other, the speculation and the newspaper stories will go on for ever. People will never quite know whether they are in love or whether they really are just good friends. So it makes sense to deny the romance.'

Melbourne businessman Chris Shannon is, however, one who *does* know the truth – for he was privileged to witness the extent of the love Jason and Kylie have had for each other for getting on for four years now. He in effect managed Jason's PAs (personal appearances) in Australia for much of that time and became very close to both young stars, watching with almost paternal pride their growing devotion to one another. It was one that led to many hilarious moments, like the time after one PA when – rarely for him – Jason had one or two of his favourite strawberry cocktails too many and decided that he wanted to see Kylie. The fact that it was 3am and she was sound asleep at her parents' house in Surrey Hills, Melbourne, made no difference. What followed was virtually straight out of a 'Scott and

Charlene' scene in 'Neighbours'.

Chris Shannon remembers, 'Jason insisted on being driven to the house, then when we got there and found it unlit and locked up he decided he would get in through an open ground-floor window. The problem was, because he had had a couple of drinks too many, he was clumsier than usual. And as he clambered in he got stuck tight, jammed absolutely solid half-in and half-out of the window. It was terrible, but so funny as well! My driver and I were pushing and pulling him, he was giggling like a madman, everyone was shouting at everyone else in whispers to be quiet in case we woke up the entire neighbourhood – if someone *had* seen us they would have called the police because we must have looked like a gang of drunk burglars! Can you imagine the headlines and scandal? Eventually, we simply put our shoulders under Jason's backside, heaved, and he popped through the window like a cork from a champagne bottle.

'He landed on the floor giggling, got up, whispered "thanks, fellas!" and wandered off to find Kylie. How she explained him away the next morning I can't imagine. I was just grateful to drive off home without feeling a policeman's hand on my collar. And there were lots of silly, fun antics like that whenever Jason and Kylie were around.'

Shannon, aware that Kylie and Jason first acted together on 'Skyways' when they were both just eleven, was in fact under the impression that the young couple were sweethearts even *before* they met up again on the 'Neighbours' set. However, Melbourne hairdresser

David Woods told an English newspaper in the summer of 1989 that he had been going out with Kylie since she was thirteen until she suddenly finished with him to go out with Jason just months after starting on 'Neighbours'.

It's a loss that still causes him pain, even though they have remained friends, and at her invitation he actually attended her twenty-first birthday party at the end of May. He says, 'She was a stunner even at thirteen and even though we did have our rows and split up a few times I had always assumed we would marry one day. Then some months after she joined 'Neighbours' she suddenly told me she wanted to finish with me. She just told me she was under such a lot of pressure from work, but I knew that wasn't the real reason. So I sat down with her a week later, insisted she told me the truth, and then she came clean about Jason. I was very hurt. Obviously, I had watched her in 'Neighbours' and seen her acting opposite him. I had asked her about him, but she said he was just another actor. I was very upset that she had deceived me, but of course I got over it. Now I am very pleased she is so happy with him, and they are very much together. She still comes into my hairdressing salon and chats and tells me how much she loves him.

'She told me how they were virtually living together for about a year, although their singing careers obviously mean that at the moment they're apart far more often than they are together. But I don't doubt that in the long run they will settle down together and marry. I hope I get an invite to the wedding! But even if I do I won't have anything to say to Jason, we have nothing in common. I have bumped into him a few times at various functions but I can't actually bring myself to speak to him because of what happened.'

Chris Shannon is another who is convinced that Jason and Kylie will wed, 'They were virtually man and wife when I knew them well anyway. I used to pick Jason up at the house he owns in Melbourne and I'd find them curled up on the sofa together in each other's arms watching TV. Or she'd be doing their washing, or cooking their dinner. As we would leave she'd ask what time he was going to be in because she wanted to know whether or not to wait up for him. Many times I dropped him off at the house late and Kylie would be asleep curled up in her nightclothes and a dressing gown on the couch. It was very sweet. They were always very lovey-dovey together in my presence, but even then they knew they had to keep their relationship undercover from the public. Jason once told me she was fed up with the secrecy and wanted to get married and come out in the open. But he knew that it would be wrong for both their careers and said no. It's just a matter of time though. One day they will get married and settle down and have a houseful of kids, I am sure. Kylie will be a natural mum, you see.'

However, there have been a few rows and hiccups in the relationship. Jason – inevitably, as he is a young, handsome, single pop and TV star – has been linked with a whole variety of beautiful women. He has also had to endure the attentions of a host of female fans who are often very reluctant to take no for an answer – one once followed him the 1,000 miles from Brisbane to Melbourne because she became deluded that she was in fact his girlfriend! She began trailing him to various personal appearances, turned up at the 'Neighbours' studio, and tried to find his home. Eventually Chris Shannon had to threaten her with legal action to make her give up.

He recalled, 'Thank goodness Kylie didn't find out about it at the time – though I think Jason told her about it later. Because the girl was very pretty, and no matter how innocent Jason was, it would have been hard for Kylie to believe there was no smoke without fire. There could be hell to play – and although Kylie is very easygoing most of the time, she has got quite a temper when she finally blows her stack. She can be very stubborn too. I remember that after they had one row they both turned up separately for a personal appearance at a nightclub, didn't say a word to each other until they went on stage, then after it was over left separately without speaking! Still, a week later it was forgotten and they were as lovey-dovey as ever.' And Kylie herself has admitted that she suffers from premenstrual tension and that that causes her to be short-tempered and 'blow her stack'.

Despite all that, they are clearly still very much in love. Both flew from opposite corners of the world back to Australia in late May 1989 to be together for their twenty-first birthday parties. Guests said that at each event both were inseparable. And a grainy but clear photograph showed them on holiday together a month later at the luxurious Hyatt Hotel on the tiny but beautiful Hawaiian island of Maui. It was their first proper holiday together since they sneaked off to Bali together two years previously. That Bali trip was a holiday they would never forget, if only because Kylie was photographed topless on a beach with Jason's arms around her waist!

5

SUPERSTAR!

Jason's first paycheck from 'Neighbours' was reported to be just $A200, or a little over £100 an episode. Three months after he started work as skateboarding Scott on the revamped, largely re-cast show the ratings were so dismal that its new owners were thinking of killing it off once and for all. It was given just six weeks to live. Actors like Jason feared they were going to have to take a paycut just to keep the show alive. It looked certain that his career as a soapstar would be over virtually before it began. Hard to believe, then, that barely two years later Jason was an international superstar raking in incredible earnings in excess of £1 million year.

Jason, looking tall, tanned and talented as he sat during the interview in Sydney's Southern Cross Hotel, could barely believe it himself. He said with a shake of his head, 'There is this legend that as soon as 'Neighbours' was relaunched with a new cast it became an instant success and within days we all became instant stars with all the benefits that brings. Nothing could be further from the truth. It was dire at the beginning, and very worrying for everyone! No one watched it at all at the beginning, far fewer in fact than watched it when it was on the previous channel! So they decided to effectively *sell* it to viewers on a door-to-door basis. They were amazing times, I can tell you. We were working a seventy to eighty hour week making the show, spending every other waking moment during the week learning lines, then at the weekend we'd be flying all over Australia promoting the show.

'Every promo device the bosses could think of, we did. I've been a prize in a newspaper competition, delivered TV sets to people nominated in a "Good Neighbours" contest, opened garden fetes, and so on. I wasn't the only one of course, all of us did it. It could be brilliant when people responded, or awful if only a handful of people bothered to turn up. But we started to notice that when we did personal appearances in shopping centres, particularly big ones in the Sydney area called Westfields, then the crowds got bigger and bigger.

'And most of them were young, my and Kylie's age or younger. We'd go out of our way to meet them and talk to them and sign autographs and so on. They seemed to like it and so did we. It was fun.'

It was also successful. Three months later the viewing figures had trebled and continued to rocket, and Jason was at last on his way to superstardom. Not that he

Jason's millions of fans treat him like royalty. Here
he makes a 'royal' balcony appearance, waving
to his fans to celebrate the success of *Ten Good
Reasons*

Half of a very private foursome: Jason and Elaine
Smith used to spend evenings together with Kylie
and Peter O'Brien. While Jason and Kylie have
gone on to pop stardom, Peter and Elaine pursue
their acting careers

Scores of fans fainted in the excitement of Jason's
half-hour personal appearance at a Glasgow
nightclub, which opened specially early so even
his younger fans would be allowed in

In a posed photograph to publicise 'Especially For You' Kylie and Jason still pretend theirs is a purely professional relationship

'Just good friends' Kylie and Jason often swop the
Australian sunshine for the chill of London
Heathrow

Fresh from success at the Amsterdam pop festival promoting *Ten Good Reasons* on satellite TV and in the media worldwide

Jason hits the Top Ten spots all over the world -
and is earning platinum and gold discs all the
time

Between them they account for millions of record sales - here are Jason and Bros during Bros's world tour on the day they arrived at the Southern Cross Hotel, Sydney in October 1988

Looking every inch a lover of the great outdoors, Jason stands by a friend's pool

In serious or light-hearted mood Jason Donovan takes a good picture! *Above*: on the set of 'Heroes', *below*: acknowledging his fans, unmistakeable even in dark glasses

had time to appreciate it; he was still working those seventy-hour weeks and racing all over Australia promoting the show. He was so hard up that he was glad to squeeze in an occasional private appearance at a local disco to judge a beauty contest and get paid $50. He still lived at home with his father, stepmother and stepbrother and drove a battered old Volkswagen his father had helped him buy.

Then one day in April 1987 he and Kylie were booked to appear on behalf of 'Neighbours' at the Royal Easter Show in Sydney. The young couple were staggered when they stepped out on stage to be confronted by an estimated 15,000 youngsters who promptly went berserk, and seemingly as one made a mad dash forwards to try and grab a piece of their heroes. Frantic police and medics had to drag to safety hundreds of young girls who were in danger of being trampled. Then those same kids would hurl themselves into the throng. Dozens were treated for hysteria and minor injuries, one young girl was rushed to hospital. Police eventually insisted that Jason and Kylie leave to avoid a serious incident – only to find they couldn't get them out. The only answer was to smuggle them clear in a sealed police 'paddy wagon'.

As Jason said, 'False modesty apart, you would have to be pretty dumb not to realise something pretty out of the ordinary was happening here. Some police guy told me he hadn't seen anything like it since the Beatles visited Australia twenty years before! And it was increasingly getting to the stage where I couldn't stroll down the streets any more with my mates or go and buy a T-shirt without getting mobbed.'

The benefits of stardom were beginning to flood in too. His salary on 'Neighbours' was tripled and requests for lucrative personal appearances began to flood in. Well-known Melbourne showbiz figure Chris Shannon became his agent for such PAs. He said, 'When "Neighbours" was first relaunched it was very difficult to find him work, frankly. He did a few, for money that was chickenfeed. The people doing the hiring were very dismissive of the show – but I persevered because I could see the kids absolutely loved him, and whenever we went back somewhere the crowds doubled from the previous visits. By the end he was making several thousand dollars a night, every night of the week if he so wanted. But just as he was starting to reach his peak the show took off in the UK. And, quite intelligently, he realised that that was where the future lay and took to spending more and more time there until he finally left 'Neighbours' and virtually emigrated to Britain.'

However, Shannon stressed, 'I have dealt with a lot of big stars in my time, both homegrown here in Australia and imported from Europe or the USA. And I have to say that Jason was an absolute joy to work with. He never became big-headed, never took off on the "I am a Star, treat me accordingly" trip. Somehow he managed to keep his feet firmly on the ground and remain a genuinely nice and straight bloke. He never began to get grandiose ideas, he stayed the same guy who was happy to stop off at a burger joint for a bite to eat rather than a posh restaurant. He'd still drink beer rather than champagne, liked to "tie one on" and go out and get drunk occasionally with his mates. When we drove back from some PA somewhere he'd take his turn at the wheel if need be, would talk about sport or clothes or cars or girls just like any guy of his age. I kept watching for him to change, he was a smashing lad but I thought that sadly it was inevitable. But he honestly never did. That's not to say he didn't get tougher, you have to. People began to grab him, tried to get a piece of the action, tried to rip him off, and so on. It goes with the territory. But with many stars it makes them paranoid, they become self-obsessed, convinced they matter above all else. They believe their own publicity. Jason never did. Frankly, we parted company because he became simply too big for me to handle. But it was totally straight and amicable. I wish to goodness all the showbiz people I have dealt with had been like him.'

Much of Jason's level-headedness, of course, came from the sensible grounding his father Terence had given him. Terry admits, 'I was determined that whatever happened he would keep his feet on the ground.

'Fame is a very powerful, heady, drug and Jason got a very powerful dose of it very young. Plus of course at that young age he began to earn far more than most grown men with families could dream of. I dinned it into him that he had to make the money work for his future, that just because it was all flooding in now there was no guarantee that it would always be that way. But I didn't have to say too much, after all he had seen the proof of that in my career. He has always been very level-headed about the ups and downs of showbusiness. He is very well aware that just because he is the flavour of the moment now that there is no guarantee that it will be that way in a month or a year or two years from now.

'I am in fact very proud of the way he handled his "Neighbours" fame. He never let it go to his head. He still phones or writes to us wherever he is in the world. He has never taken advantage of his position as a star for youngsters. He could have been out on the town every night with a different girl, driving a flash car, got raging drunk, accepted the drugs I am sure would be available if he wanted them. He has done none of that. He only really left home because I pushed him into it thinking that for financial reasons it made sense to buy his own place. Even then it wasn't anywhere flash, it was a rundown place that we could do up and make money on. We've both got a lot of satisfaction out of doing most of the physical work ourselves. He is proud of it, and rightly so. But he still comes home to us when he needs a rest and he loves to call in on Sunday for his stepmum Marlene's roast!'

In fact, Jason is now starting to splash out more. He recently bought a second, bigger house in Central Melbourne and is in the process of selling the first place in Gibden Street, Burnley, Melbourne. Again it is an investment and he and his father will start the renovations soon. Like the first house, it will be light and airy, with soft pastel shades rather than striking decor. He likes furniture simple, functional and comfortable rather than merely fashionable. Another must is a well-stocked kitchen, for Jason likes to cook for himself. But washing-up is no favourite, so he has splashed out on a

Jason's first house in Gibden St, Burnley,
Melbourne

dishwasher. Jason has also bought himself a new Range-
Rover, to go with the seven-year-old Volkswagen Golf he
has had for so long. He is well aware of how much he
owes to his fans, and never complains when they
approach and ask him for autographs. If he can he stops
and chats. Except, that is, if they turn up on his doorstep.
He has a firm rule about that. Similarly, all of his mail is
diverted from his or his father's house to his manager
Richard East's office.

As Jason explained, 'Frankly, there is so much of it
it would be impossible to cope with. But I do try to

ensure that as much as possible of it gets answered. And it might surprise people how much of it I do actually read. I think you have to, after all these are the people who have made you this thing called 'a star' and if you forget that then you are in trouble.'

6

FROM RAMSAY STREET TO HIT PARADE

The road from Ramsay Street to the Hit Parade was much more difficult for Jason Donovan than virtually anyone would suspect. There were many hurdles to overcome on the way – not least his own sense of pride. He had to face, and not be intimidated by, constant accusations that he was only doing it because he was jealous of his girlfriend Kylie's amazing transition from being a soap opera celebrity to international singing star. But what kept him going was a deep inner conviction that he really did have a singing talent and that he was born to make music. The proof of how right he was to persevere is the fact that by Christmas 1989 industry experts believe he will have sold an astonishing 10 *million* singles and albums worldwide. He has already achieved Top Ten chart successes in eighteen countries (see end of chapter) around the globe and made himself a millionare several times over. And in the summer of 1989 he signed an estimated £1.5m deal to release his records in the biggest marketplace of them all, the USA. Not bad for a bloke the Australian press once tried to rubbish as a singing no-hoper who was simply trying to copycat Kylie! In fact Jason was approached to make a record *before* Kylie, and by the same people who were later to snap her up. Michael Gudinski of Australia's Mushroom Records suggested to the rising young 'Neighbours' star that he cut a record a year after he joined the show. Neither party denies very strongly that it was aimed at cashing in on Jason's 'Neighbours' fame and would have been a short-term project – just as the 'Neighbours' cast cut a 'Neighbours' record for the 1988 Christmas novelty market. But it was for that very reason that Jason thought long and hard and then turned them down flat. He was absolutely entranced with the possibility of becoming a popstar and didn't want to waste what he knew was a golden opportunity.

He was shrewd enough to know that if he released a poor first record, any further attempt at a pop career would never be taken seriously. So instead, he went back home and began teaching himself all over again the music that he had learnt as a schoolboy in Melbourne's Melba Conservatory of Music and in the Australian Boys' Choir. Two years later, he was chatting to Michael Gudinski at a showbiz function and he was asked whether he had reconsidered a recording career. This time he said he would give it a go.

By now Gudinski had established close links via his singing protegée Kylie Minogue with that English pop success machine S.A.W., run by those three record producers with the golden touch, Mike Stock, Matt Aitken and Pete Waterman. So it was agreed that during one of his many 'Neighbours' promotional trips to Britain Jason would slip into their recording studio in London and record two demo tapes – one of them a cover of a track on one of Jason's favourite albums by the band Noiseworks. Jason has admitted, 'I was still very, very nervous, and it wasn't brilliant. I was on tenterhooks to see what they'd say. Finally Peter Waterman had a good listen and decided that there was something there to work on. That gave my confidence the boost it needed. I was really scared of being such a novice working with such major people in the pop industry.'

Pete Waterman recalls, 'He *was* a novice, he was very nervous, but I didn't really have any doubts. He did have talent, so I knew we had a goldseam to work on. And we were proved right very quickly. We had the know-how to bring out what the world now accepts was there.

'All the sniping and knocking Jason had to put up with was tough on him, but we told him to just ignore it and enjoy himself. And he learnt the business so quickly. He is a joy to work with. We told him what he had to do and he knuckled down and he did it. The results are obvious. We explained that having a successful pop career today isn't just about cutting a record and letting it take its chances on the radio station's playlists, you have to promote and work at it. He understood, perhaps as a result of what happened in the early days of 'Neighbours', the sense in that. He's never looked back since.'

Then, after months of anticipation, in September 1988 his first single was released, called 'Nothing Can Divide Us'. It was an instant success around the world, hitting the Top Five in both Britain and Australia. It sold a massive 540,000 copies worldwide, making it go gold very quickly. His next effort, 'Especially For You', a romantic duet with girlfriend Kylie aimed at the Christmas market, rocketed to Number One. In all it sold 830,000 copies in Britain alone, a staggering 2,660,000 around the world.

Record sales like these, quite apart from the pleasure and joy he got from succeeding in a second career, also brought him a king's ransom of an income. He is estimated to have earned an enormous £348,000 in the first six months of his pop career alone.

However, that very success forced Jason into a corner. He knew that he couldn't sustain his new pop career while at the same time continuing to meet the frantic demands of the 'Neighbours' schedule. One or other had to go. But he had been getting restless with 'Neighbours' for a long time. He had demanded – and got – a long break from the show to be allowed to make the highly successful TV mini-series 'Heroes' which was screened both in the UK and Australia.

TV bosses had also boosted his salary to $120,000 a year in an attempt to keep him happy. Not bad considering the very modest salary he started on. But it was no good. Jason reluctantly decided 'Neighbours' had to go.

In early 1989 Jason was back in Britain to release a new single, 'Too Many Broken Hearts'. Several months later he was back home in Melbourne asleep when at 6am one morning the phone rang. It was his manager Richard East to tell him he had just pushed passed Madonna to hit his first Number One. Jason recalled, 'It was the most fantastic feeling. I just lay there and said "wow!".' The single went on to sell a million copies worldwide, importantly most of those *outside* Britain and Australia. It proved that his singing appeal wasn't limited to those countries where the public knew him first as Scott from 'Neighbours'. They were buying the records because they liked them, not just because he was a TV star. On that same trip that Jason recorded 'Too Many Broken Hearts' he began recording his first album. It was finally finished out in Australia when Stock and Aitken flew out to put the finishing touches to it in a Melbourne studio.

Next came Jason's single 'Sealed With a Kiss', which entered the charts at Number One in both Britain and Australia, the first time an Australian has ever achieved that. Again, sales worldwide were massive. In Britain alone they totalled an estimated 1,350,000. Jason's first album, called *Ten Good Reasons*, came out that summer and also shot straight to Number One in the LP charts. His record company revealed that as expected it sold over a million copies worldwide – netting him a huge £800,000. In other words, Jason's pop experiment has left him in the happy position of never needing to work again.

However, as he says, 'Money has never been the issue. That wasn't why I left "Neighbours" or why I went into a singing career. What mattered was the challenge and being a success. I want to be the best at whatever I do. I would have wanted to be the best plumber or carpenter or designer if my career had gone that way rather than in show business.

'And despite all the pop success I will never give up acting. In fact later in 1989 or early 1990 I am definitely going to do a film project with my dad in Australia that will probably take two or three months. There has also been a whole host of other films and TV offers both in Australia and Britain which I am considering. But for a while at least the pop career will come first. My main priority at the moment is putting together a stage show for me to take on a tour of concert dates.'

In fact, Jason plans to do that first tour of Britain in February and March 1990. He may then add some dates in Europe. He is also deeply interested in expanding to the USA, as his £1.5 million American contract proves. It is an area where Kylie has already shown Jason it is possible to succeed.

Early in 1989 Jason did a promotional mini-tour of Britain, appearing in nightclubs miming to his hit records and meeting the fans – who went wild for him. There was such hysteria that police had to call off several appearances, and several thousand youngsters had to be given medical assistance. Experienced tour organiser Tony McGarahan spluttered afterwards, 'What is it with this kid? I've been on all these dates and I've never seen anything like it, it's like Beatlemania four times over, there were even young girls trying to bottle the air that he'd breathed at one concert! Yet Jason is such a great sweet bloke. I have seen a lot of big name stars, but I

Cap that! Jason clearly enjoyed his schooldays,
and to this day his father treasures his uniform

reckon this guy will just go on and on getting better.'

After the nightclub tour Jason slipped back home to Australia to celebrate with Kylie their twenty-first birthdays – they were born just three days apart. Then it was off to Japan for a short promotional tour, before returning to the UK via a business trip to New York. Despite his two homes in Melbourne, Jason was planning to buy a £250,000 home in central London. Something told him he would need a permanent base there.

WORLDWIDE SUCCESS: Jason has hit the Top Ten in all these countries (mainly with 'Too Many Broken Hearts', 'Especially for You', and his album *Ten Good Reasons*):

Portugal	Norway
Eire	Sweden
Spain	Finland
UK	Hong Kong
Holland	Australia
Germany	New Zealand
Greece	Belgium
Switzerland	Israel
Austria	Denmark

7

DO YOU REALLY KNOW JASON?

Jason Donovan has had one of the most extraordinary rises to superstardom that show business has ever seen. Here are Twenty Things that you probably didn't know about him.

1 Jason loves to grab a few moments alone with girlfriend Kylie Minogue – but even so he could have done without their enforced time together when they got trapped alone for almost thirty minutes in a stuck lift on their way to a swish awards ceremony at a top Melbourne hotel. It was made worse because Jason suffers mildly from claustrophobia.

2 Both Jason and Kylie had to be smuggled out of a New South Wales shopping centre in a laundry van hidden under sacks of dirty towels when ten times more

'Neighbours' fans than expected turned up to see them make a personal appearance. It happened a week before their 'marriage' as Scott Robinson and Charlene Mitchell was screened on TV. But it was even worse a week after the TV wedding – security guards and police had to fight through a sea of over-excited fans at a Sydney shopping complex to get the couple to safety.

3 Jason hysteria in Britain became so crazy that besotted fans started taking jars to concerts and appearances to try to bottle the air that he breathed! Britain's top-selling newspaper the *Sun* spotted the craze and actually ran a light-hearted contest for readers to win a sealed bottle of the great man's breath – and the paper was astonished to receive thousands of entries.

4 One of the first things Jason bought when he began spending a lot of time in Britain was a fruit blender. He complained that you couldn't get proper fresh fruit juices so decided to make his own. And the one thing his record company know they must do before all else is to ensure he always has a supply of oranges, grapefruit and apples for him to make fresh drinks.

5 He is a Gemini – born at exactly 6pm on Saturday 1 June 1968. Astrologers who have read his chart say he is an incurable romantic, but prefers brains to empty-headed beauty; he is a great talker and loves gossip, but is very quick at spotting people trying to flannel him; he loves luxury, likes making money, and is almost over-generous to those close to him – but he isn't ostentatious

with cash and prefers not to spend it on himself; he has great imagination but is also very practical with his hands and would have made a great car mechanic!

6 He absolutely loathes wearing any kind of shoes. If he had his way he would go barefoot everywhere. But once he does find shoes that are comfortable he wears them until they drop to pieces – like the pair of cowboy boots he bought in New York, which he wore in the pro-motional video for his hit single 'Too Many Broken Hearts'.

7 His favourite actor is Michael Douglas; Jack Nicholson in *Batman* and *The Witches of Eastwick* comes a close second. He also rates Michael J. Fox. Favourite actresses are Meryl Streep, Jodie Foster in *The Accused*, and some Aussie unknown called Kylie Minogue in just about anything!

8 More than 2,000 fan letters a week poured in when Jason starred as Scott in 'Neighbours' – but the figure doubled when he turned popstar as well.

9 To keep fit Jason jogs five miles every day, goes swimming for thirty minutes five times a week, works out with weights whenever he can, and does fifty press-ups followed by fifty sit-ups every morning. No wonder 5ft 11ins tall Jason weighs a trim 10st 7lbs!

10 Swimming fanatic Jason once thought he was going to be eaten by sharks when he paddled out into the deep

off a famous Australian resort called Surfers Paradise. He recalls, 'I could see these shadows in the water and I thought "hell, sharks! I am about to die" but then these things flew out of the water – they were dolphins! I almost cried with happiness and relief.'

11 Jason narrowly missed death a second time when he made his first solo trip to Los Angeles on holiday. He was in a taxi waiting at a red light when an out-of-control refuse truck whose brakes had failed missed ploughing into them by inches. But it ploughed into the car in front and killed the passengers outright. Jason recalls, 'Another couple of feet and I'd have been dead. But God and luck were on my side. It was like something from a movie happening in slow motion.'

12 It's tough to be a 'Neighbours' star – during his three years on the show Jason got accidentally knocked out when a supposedly fake punch from Kylie connected with his jaw; he nearly drowned for real when he got cramp during a fictional drowning scene; and while filming scenes at Melbourne's Luna Park funfair he got stuck seventy-five feet in the air in a howling gale on a big dipper for fifteen minutes when the machinery jammed.

13 Jason is a superstar throughout most of the world – but that didn't stop a prestigious Australian magazine, *The Bulletin*, from including him in a list of Australia's 100 Most Appalling People. They dismissed him as a "flaxen-haired warbler, a flop".

First days of 'Neighbours' fame: one of Jason's
early pin-up photos

14 Hard to believe, but squeaky-clean Jason once admitted to being a shoplifter. He explained he was about eleven at the time: 'I stole a few things from the local newsagent, all my pals did. It's part of growing up as much as anything else. I am sure that most kids have nicked something at one time or another and I was no different.'

15 Jason was immensely proud to be picked to star in the dramatic TV mini-series 'Heroes' – but then was knocked sideways to receive a letter telling him his part was to be virtually axed! He was heartbroken for a day, until a practical joking friend felt sorry for him and confessed it was a hoax. Co-star Cameron Daddo, who first met Jason when they were both in 'Neighbours', recalls, 'I managed to get some writing paper with "The Heroes" letterhead and wrote a note from the director to Jason saying his part was to be drastically cut. He came rushing into me in a blind panic. I let him sweat for a while, then put him out of his misery.'

16 Two muggers were left battered, bruised and empty-handed after they tried to steal a suitcase from Jason late one night. It happened in Notting Hill, West London, after Jason got out of a cab and was paying off the driver. Two men shoved him to one side, grabbed the case and hared off. But Jason set off in pursuit without a moment's thought, flattened both robbers with just one punch apiece, and got his bag back.

17 Jason's all-time favourite holiday spot is the luxury

Hyatt Hotel on the paradise isle of Maui in Hawaii. It is built around a lagoon where from your room you can watch whales and dolphins swim and play. Second favourite is Bali – where he was snapped having a fun time with topless Kylie.

18 Jasonmania brought a teenage fan Catherine Smithson from Staffordshire back from the dead after she went into a deadly coma following a car crash. To try to bring the nineteen-year-old girl round her mother Judith played her Jason's records constantly. It didn't seem to work until her mother switched the tapes off – and Catherine woke up to complain.

19 An estimated 2,270 teenage girls fainted and needed to be revived by medical attendants during a whirlwind promotional tour of nightclubs in Britain by Jason. Doctors estimated that at one personal appearance in Newcastle-upon-Tyne a girl was collapsing every twelve seconds!

20 Jason is a Beatles fanatic – the very first album he ever bought was a box set of their earliest albums. Though it still has pride of place in his record collection, it has now been joined by INXS, George Michael, New Order, Bruce Springsteen and Rick Astley.

Jason poses at a London waxworks museum with
a wax 'John Lennon' at the opening of a Beatles
tableau

20 QUICK TEASERS TEST

1 What is Jason Donovan's middle name? (Clue: He is of Irish extraction).

2 Name the six TV shows Jason acted in before 'Neighbours'.

3 What is the name of the prestigious award Jason won for being Australia's Most Popular Actor?

4 Which song was played at Scott and Charlene's wedding in 'Neighbours'?

5 What is Jason's favourite city in the world?

6 Which solo single record was Jason's first Number One in Britain?

7 Who have written all of Jason's hit songs?

8 Which actor first played Scott Robinson in 'Neighbours'?

9 What is Jason's favourite food?

10 When was Jason's song 'Sealed With A Kiss' first recorded and who by?

11 What was the part Jason was first offered in 'Neighbours'?

12 What is Jason's Australian record label called?

13 What are Jason and Kylie's star signs?

14 Jason had two pet poodles as a youngster – can you name them?

15 What are Jason's three favourite sports?

16 How much does Jason weigh and how tall is he?

17 On what date was Jason's first album *Ten Good Reasons* released in Britain?

18 What was Jason's first single release and what number in the British charts did it reach?

19 What was Jason's first house in Gibden St, Burnley, Melbourne, before it was converted into living accommodation?

20 What was the name of the character Jason played in his first TV mini-series 'Heroes'?

ANSWERS

1 Sean
2 'The Crawfords', 'Home', 'Golden Pennies', 'I Can Jump Puddles', 'Marshland' and 'Skyways'
3 The Silver Logie
4 'Suddenly', by Angry Anderson
5 New York
6 'Too Many Broken Hearts'
7 Mike Stock, Matt Aitken and Pete Waterman
8 Darius Perkins
9 Bread – as toast, with butter, with garlic, in sandwiches, even bread'n'butter pudding!
10 1960, Brian Highland
11 Danny Ramsay
12 Mushroom Records

13 They're both Gemini. He was born at 6pm on Saturday, 1 June 1968, she came into the world just three days earlier
14 Abby and Benji
15 Surfing, swimming and skateboarding
16 10st 7lbs, and 5ft 11ins tall
17 20 April 1989
18 'Nothing Can Divide Us', and it peaked at Number Five
19 It was an old Methodist chapel
20 'Happy' Huston

8

JASON - THE FUTURE

When you have only recently turned twenty-one, are worth millions of pounds, go out with a gorgeous girl who is also an international star, have had a bunch of Number One pop records around the globe, and are a famous TV actor on both sides of the world, what the dickens do you do next? As Jason said on a British TV programme in the summer of 1989, 'Just keep trying to get better and better, becoming more and more successful as time goes by.'

But it really is a poser that Jason Donovan faces as he looks towards the 1990s. Fortunately, Jason has surrounded himself with a bunch of close advisors whose aim is to make sure he really does get bigger and better in the years to come – primarily, of course, as a rock and pop star. But, in a typical example of how Jason has got an old head on his young shoulders, he is making

Playing seventeen-year-old 'Happy' Huston in
'Heroes' made Jason think seriously about his life
and career

wise decisions as an actor too. For example, in 'Neighbours', Jason left the show in Australia early 1989 (though he will continue appearing in the soap opera on British screens for most of 1990) but has left the door open for a return appearance.

His character Scott disappeared to Queensland, trying to save his marriage to Charlene (real-life girlfriend Kylie Minogue) who had fled there wracked with guilt and shame after secretly having a fling with a man at the garage where she worked. Her ostensible reason was that her father was ill and she wanted to help look after him. Scott played along with the separation for a while, burying himself in his new career as a trainee journalist with his local paper, the *Erinsborough News*. But then in the course of researching an article on the local Greek community he meets a beautiful young Greek girl who agrees to become his interpreter.

At first they are just friends, as they spend a lot of time working late into the night on the project. But slowly the girl begins to fall in love with Scott. Her father spots it and gets very angry because Scott has never hidden the fact he is married. The beautiful black-eyed girl goes to Ramsay Street for a swim with Jason one afternoon. As she shows off her attractive figure in a skimpy swimming costume, Scott begins to realise that he, too, is falling in love. Wracked with guilt in turn, he fights down his feelings and decides to up sticks and follow Charlene to Queensland to try and save his marriage.

So both Jason and Kylie left 'Neighbours' in such a way that if all their other career interests flopped at once they could return to the superhit show and be welcomed with open arms. In fact, insiders suggest that Jason has already had quiet discussions to allow him to make sudden short guest appearances down Ramsay Street later in 1990 if he can fit them in. The plan would be that he returns to see his father Jim Robinson (played by Alan Dale) to talk about problems in his marriage to Charlene and – surprise – has a brief flirtation with latest 'Neighbours' beauty Rachel Friend. But, that is still very much up in the air.

What is much more certain is that Jason is determined to try and break into movies in a major way. He was a great hit in the very successful mini-series 'Heroes' when, thanks to his youthful looks, he played seventeen-year-old commando 'Happy' Huston. It was a very physically draining and taxing role, filmed in some of the toughest areas of North-Eastern Australia near the Great Barrier Reef. Shortly afterwards Jason said, 'In a very real sense, in several ways, making that mini-series changed my life. It made me realise just how safe and easy my life really was. That was a real-life World War Two story in which this seventeen-year-old I was playing risked life and limb for three months to launch an amazingly daring operation against the Japanese in Singapore. It made me look twice at just how cosy and risk-free my world was. It also toughened me up physically, too, because we had to try and get as tough as those guys simply to do some of the stuff they did – like paddling canoes for hours on end! My hands were blistered, my feet were blistered, my legs ached, I seemed to be permanently exhausted. But in a way I felt better than I had ever done.'

It also reassured him he *was* capable of more stretching acting than he had ever done in 'Neighbours'. He became determined to do another such role as soon as possible. Which is why he will, in later 1989 and early 1990, travel north from Melbourne once again to make his first movie. Again it is an adventure drama – though details are being kept secret for the time being – called 'Two Years In A Tin-Can'.

It also gives him a chance to work for the first time with his actor father Terence Donovan, now one of the most respected men in Australian show-business circles. Terry has not only raised the £3m cash to finance the film, but will co-direct it and star in it alongside his famous son. It is a family affair that will be a certain blockbuster both Down Under and in Europe for 1990.

But it will mean Jason taking a hefty slice out of his pop music schedule, just when that is at boiling point. The biggest single item on that agenda is to try to take the USA by the same sort of storm with which he's conquered Australia and Britain. His estimated £1.5million two-year record deal is with record industry giants Atlantic Records, so there is a lot riding on his success.

By happy coincidence, Grundy Television of Australia – who own the rights to 'Neighbours' – had recently completed a major deal to sell the show to many cable television stations spread all across the USA. That cannot help but assist Jason when he makes his first attempts to conquer North America late in 1989 and early 1990 – in between making that movie with his father. He will also be slotting in lengthy trips to the UK, where he once rented a £250,000 luxury apartment on a long lease right in the heart of London's trendy Kensington. He will be in Britain recording a new album with Stock, Aitken and Waterman, with the aim of releasing it for the Christmas market. He also intends to release a Christmas single, hoping to reach the coveted Number One spot he grabbed with Kylie with 'Especially For You' in 1988.

Insiders within Jason's private management company, Seal Rocks Ltd, have revealed that the next major move after that will be Jason's first concert tour of Britain and Europe, which is pencilled in for spring 1990. It will be staged at major venues in most of Britain's big cities. There will also be live TV appearances in Germany, Holland and Belgium, and plans are being made for live broadcasts on satellite TV in Britain. If the hysteria that resulted from his Personal Appearance tour of Britain in early summer 1989 is anything to go by – when more than 2,000 fans had to have medical treatment for fainting – it will be a blockbuster!

Jason's family life is also happier than ever before. In early 1989 Jason confirmed that he had built bridges with, and re-established close contact with, his estranged mother Sue McIntosh. It happened after Jason bumped into his stepfather at the 'Neighbours' studio.

After an awkward silence they got chatting, and he was invited to ring his mother. Worried both by the reception he might get and also by what his father might think, Jason brooded on it for several days. Though Terence Donovan remains bitter about his ex-wife he said, 'My feelings towards the woman and what she did haven't changed. Why should they? As a child, my son was terribly hurt by her rejection. However, as a man he wanted to move on and grow by sorting out his feelings. The only way he could do that was by re-establishing contact with her. Of course, he was worried that by doing that it would hurt me. But although it was still painful to me I understand that there is only one mother in a person's life and we should all make the best of it. So I told him to get back in touch. The situation was a minefield for him, so I helped him to cross it.

'Not surprisingly, he was scared it could all end up in rejection again. I am glad to say that that hasn't happened, and that there are no signs that it will. I just pray it will continue that way.'

Jason described the emotional meeting, 'My mother invited me over to the house and it was wonderful to see my three little half-sisters. There is Katherine who is almost fourteen, Olivia who is twelve, and the baby of the family Stephanie aged three. We all got along so well. It somehow seemed the easiest and most natural thing in the world to do. I get on so well with them all, but it has not affected my relationship with my dad and stepmum Marlene and my little brother Paul at all. Suddenly my family is doubled. It is so great that my family life has come good along with everything else in my world. I am a very lucky guy.'